MW00563657

APERÇUS

APERÇUS
The Aphorisms of
MIGNON
MCLAUGHLIN

Introduction by Josh Michaels

© Thomas Paine McLaughlin, aphorisms from *The Second Neurotic's Notebook;* photographs

© The Brabant Press, Introduction

cover design: Kachergis Book Design

cover photo: Mignon McLaughlin, 1965; Frances McLaughlin-Gill

typesetting: Diane Collins

TABLE OF CONTENTS

INTRODUCTION

Mignon McLaughlin was born in Baltimore on June 6, 1913, the only child of a Jewish couple, attorney Hyman Bushel (1891–1969) and his wife Joyce Cohen (1892–1975). Hyman had emigrated from Russia in 1898; Joyce's family had arrived from the Rhineland two generations earlier, in the mid-19th century. Her father, Jacob, raised in Brooklyn, served as a customs inspector for nearly fifty years.

When Mignon was three or four, the Bushels returned to New York—Hyman had grown up there as well—and divorced soon after. Mignon saw little or nothing of her father after age seven. He eventually moved to Massachusetts and became a magistrate.

Like her husband, Joyce was a lawyer, and joined the New York State Bar Association. She soon remarried, and her criminal law practice flourished. Now Joyce Neuhaus, she was a canny investor and, perhaps the beneficiary of inside information, got out of the stock market before the Crash. She had an apartment on the Upper West Side, 640 Riverside Drive, and an office on Broadway. By the mid-'40s Joyce had divorced and re-married again. Husband number three (or four) was Milton Kolb, a civil engineer, and the couple bought a home in exclusive Point Lookout, Long Island. Joyce could be domineering and manipulative, and she and her daughter had a falling-out at some point during the '50s.

i

Mignon, always called Mike, was petite and precocious, with a sly sense of humor. She was an avid reader and majored in English when she entered Smith College in 1929. A mentor at Smith was Mina Kirstein Curtiss, editor of Proust's letters and a well-known, and well-connected, memoirist. Curtiss may have helped McLaughlin land a position as a features writer at Hearst's *New York American* after she graduated in 1933. Three years later McLaughlin married Loren Disney (no relation to Walt, she assured her sons). The couple divorced within a few years. By 1940 she was living in a crowded lodging house in Greenwich Village, listing her occupation as "writer."

But the '40s turned out to be a golden decade for Mignon. At the end August 1941, she married Robert McLaughlin (1908-1973) a short, boyish-looking editor at *McCall's*, with sharp features and penetrating brown eyes. Robert was from Chicago, and his family was also well-off: his father, Frank, Jr., owned a profitable fuel company that was not much affected by the Depression.

After dropping out of University of Colorado, Robert had joined the staff of the *Rocky Mountain News* and had then moved to *Time* before becoming the managing editor of *McCall's*. At the beginning of 1943, he was inducted into the army. As with so many other aspiring novelists, the war proved a godsend. Though he did not see combat or even go abroad—he served for the duration at Edgewood Arsenal in Baltimore, where he edited *Chemical Warfare Bulletin*— Lieutenant McLaughlin parleyed his experiences, and what he'd heard, into terse, Hemmingwayesque short stories that were published in *The New Yorker*. These appeared as a collection in 1945, *A Short Wait Between Trains*. The title story, about African-American soldiers forced to eat in the kitchen in a small southern town, while German p.o.w.s were served in the lunch room, based on a real incident, excited much attention. In other stories, platoons of carefully mixed ethnicities, classes, and regions (the Poles tell their rosaries, the Southerners swill their bourbon) go through non-combat experiences that nonetheless test and bind them.

McLaughlin then published a long, ambitious novel, also with Knopf and with a World War II setting, about a conflict between two Irish-American brothers, a liberal idealist and a cynical hedonist and conservative. Though inevitably dated, as any *roman à these*—there are extended political and philosophical debates between the brothers, and their friends and lovers—*The Side of the Angels* (1947) is well-written and absorbing, and, as first novels often do, reveals something about the author and, in this case, his wife.

The character who appears to be based on Mignon is described as "small and dark and having a gamin look." She has "very nice eyes, brown and faintly slanted." The protagonist, the younger brother, Tom, "liked the way she looked. She was small and well formed and had smooth olive skin and quite strange eyes, wide-spaced and oddly slanted... Her nose was straight and her mouth rather full." When he asks if she's Eurasian, she tells him, "In some people's book I am. I'm a Jew."

She is also combative. When she doesn't like a ditty that her host recites about Roosevelt, she spills her martini in his lap. The character grew up in a prosperous, assimilated Jewish family in Baltimore, and loathes the city. ("Baltimore's coat of arms should represent snobbism rampant on a field of racial hate.") Like Tom, she has strong left-wing sympathies, but is more outspoken. "Making a living from the products of other men's labor does something ruinous to a man," she declares, a little tactlessly, after Tom has told her about his father's suicide.

He asked curiously, "Are you a Commie?"

"No," she said.

"What are you?"

She smiled grimly. "Incoherent."

He laughed. "No, tell me."

"I'm a New Dealer, I guess. A starry-eyed idealist..."

A little later she confesses, "I don't know anything. When I realize how little I know—about Marxism, about capitalism, about anything political—I feel like crying. I just want people to be good to each other; it's as simple as that."

Mignon, meanwhile, had become an editor at *Vogue* and was publishing short stories in women's magazines–*Cosmopolitan*, *Red Book*, and, especially, *Good Housekeeping*. At least a dozen appeared during the decade. Nineteen-forty-six was a banner year, with two that ran in two parts in successive issues, and another she described as a short novel. But if she made efforts to interest a publisher—as she must have done—these were not successful.

The stories range in quality, though the plots are inevitably formulaic. In a couple of the less contrived narratives, the protagonist is a young woman working in an advertising agency in New York. In the two-part story "Illusion," a shy office manager, Martha Evans, is infatuated with one of her bosses, the dashing lady-killer Colby Devereux, goes to charm school, loses twenty pounds, and succeeds in interesting him. But the chance arrival of his mistress, a supermodel, at the restaurant where he's taken Martha spoils the assignation, and she winds up marrying the rumpled, bookish widower next door, a museum curator. She has a baby and is happy with her lot. After learning of the suicide of the model, Martha is even more grateful to have escaped the fast lane—a denouement no doubt entirely satisfying to readers of *Good Housekeeping*. This is a theme that recurs in other stories: a small-town girl comes to the metropolis, is smitten with a debonair playboy, but winds up with a wholesome, reliable type, with small-town values—but who has the intelligence and sense of humor the native beaus had lacked.

"That's How It Was" has more sparkle. It's the story of a pretty, popular girl from a small town in Ohio, Dinah Linthrop, who, by chance, befriends an unconventional girl not part of her crowd, Isobel Brewster, and is persuaded to escape Cartersville and her arrogant and boring fiancée. The depiction of Isobel, of a bitter schoolteacher, and of Dinah's shrewd father enliven the narrative, and there are occasional *mots* that anticipate the *Notebooks*, though the plot heads south when Dinah and Isobel go east to New York.

One of McLaughlin's last publications of the decade, "You Remember Elaine," marks a further transition from storyteller to aphorist—but for this reason the narrative is still less satisfying. Told from a male point of view, it concerns a husband, a successful businessman, who has always regarded his first wife as the guardian of his conscience, and his divorce the result of his turning his back on his youthful ideals. When he meets her again, he sees that she was reproaching him only because this was his vulnerable point; with her second husband, it's his weight. He has a surge of warm feelings for his second wife, whom he'd come to think of as shallow and materialistic.

Only one story is set in Baltimore, "That's How It Was." But there are no Jewish characters, nor in any other story—there hardly could be, given the audience she was writing for. The narrator, Georgia Wilson, has married into a socially prominent Baltimore family, and makes some astringent observations on her wealthy in-laws and their friends. In some ways the most accomplished of McLaughlin's stories, "That's How It Was" includes some intriguing characters, including an infatuated neighbor dominated by his wife and a dapper, closeted homosexual suitor. ("A generation earlier he would have been called 'effete.' Now he was considered 'amusing.'") In the end, like so many McLaughlin heroines, Georgia escapes to New York, where it appears as if she will be re-united with her former husband Ridge, a doctor who had divorced her in part I.

Less successful are mid-decade attempts at a noir mystery, a short novel called *Sins of the Father*, and a quasi-political thriller, the two-part "The Governor's Lady."

Late in the decade, Mignon and Robert began collaborating on plays. In early 1947 or '48, she contacted Mina Curtiss, asking if her former teacher recalled a particular passage from D. H. Lawrence on love that would be appropriate in a scene between "a sweet but rather dopey young girl" and "an extremely bright and sophisticated young man." (In her breathless letter, Mignon misspelled not only Curtiss's name, but her own maiden name as well.) Jed Harris was to direct the play, and it was to open in February. The deal fell apart, though, and it was never produced.

But then in May 1949, a play by the McLaughlins opened on Broadway, *Gayden*, produced by their friend Josh Logan. Mignon described it as "a suspenseful character study of a psychopathic son living cruelly and in pampered luxury with his unsuspecting and doting mother." The play starred Fay Bainter, a well-know actress in '40s, and a miscast Jay Robinson, rumored to be the boyfriend of the director. Robinson, according to IMDB, "owned a pair of the narrowest, cruelest-looking eyes in 1950s Hollywood. To compliment them was an evil-looking sneer, crisp and biting diction and a nefarious-sounding cackle." This worked for Caligula in *The Robe*, but not for Gayden, who was supposed to be manipulative but somewhat sympathetic. The play closed after eight nights, the last two to nearly empty houses.

The waters of Lethe closed over it, though the couple's oldest son loyally revived it in a college production in the mid-'60s.

There would be no more plays after *Gayden* and only a single story publication after 1948. But at some point in the '50s McLaughlin found her métier—pithy, humorous observations. The first batch appeared as "Punundrums" in *Redbook* in February 1958. In the early '60s, she published three selections in *Atlantic*, one a full page, the others less, under the title "The Neurotic's Notebook." These and other *aperçus* were published in 1963 by Bobbs-Merrill. A second compendium appeared in 1966. They were issued together as a gift set two years later, and in 1981 a small house, Castle Books, re-published the collection, with recurring crude marginal drawings of no relevance to the aphorisms, which must have annoyed the author.

In the '40s McLaughlin also became a mother. In February 1944, Robert and Mignon adopted a son, whom they named Thomas Paine, and a second, James Joyce, in March of 1945. "A marriage without children is like a Chinese dinner without rice," she had decided. "The flavor may be there, but not the substance."

As is clear from a number of other aphorisms, she enjoyed her family. "If your children spend most of their time in other people's houses, you're lucky; if they all congregate in your house, you're blessed." She seems to have been so blessed, despite—or because—her children didn't share her sensibility: "Sarcasm, like haemophilia, is transmitted by the females of the family." "We don't mind our children having different virtues from ours, but it seems disloyal of them to have different faults."

Some aphorists are morose and meditative, but Mignon, by all accounts, was bubbly and gregarious, with a lightning wit and infectious laugh. "She had a mouth on her," one friend recalled. Some of her aphorisms no doubt originated as extemporaneous quips.

The McLaughlins were denizens in good standing of the New York literary and entertainment world. Among their friends were Neil Simon, Mel Brooks, Reginald Rose, Teddy White, Sid Caesar, Carl Reiner, and Tony Randall and their wives, ex-wives, and girlfriends, along with leading editors and publishers. The world of publishing, then perhaps even more so than now, was lubricated by alcohol. There was an endless round of cocktail parties, openings, receptions, and shows, apart from the liquid lunches over which deals were made and broken.

Both Robert and Mignon drank heavily and she was a chain-smoker. ("Cigarettes are all the clock I need: one pack finishes the morning, another the afternoon, a third the night." "Good food, good sex, good digestion, good sleep: to these basic animal pleasures man has added nothing but the good cigarette.") Mignon also used barbiturates ("The only patience the neurotic knows is that to be found in a bottle of sleeping pills.") and occasionally gambled. ("The gambling fever, once it has passed, is as impossible to remember as pain.") Friends of her younger son recall the couple retiring upstairs at their brownstone off 51st and 1st Avenue with a bottle of scotch and a quart of milk, while they had the run of the rest of the house. Summers were spent at a bungalow in Fair Harbor on Fire Island, then a writers' enclave, and a hotbed of promiscuous socializing and occasional partner-swapping.

The Side of the Angels was admired by reviewers, but didn't sell as well as Robert or his publisher had anticipated. He had resigned from *McCall's* after he was demobilized and hoped to be able to write full time. The McLaughlins moved to Newburyport, Massachusetts in 1947. But the following year Robert accepted a position as an editor at *Time*, and the couple returned to Manhattan. He would remain with the magazine for two decades. His second novel would not appear for a dozen years, *The Notion of Sin* (1959), followed two years later by *The Walls of Heaven* (1961). Both went through three editions, but there was no break-through for Robert into the ranks of the major contemporary American novelists. A final non-fiction book about the Midwest, published in the Time-Life Library of America, also did well: *The Heartland* (1968). McLaughlin turned down repeated offers of promotion to Senior Editor at *Time*. As a Contributing Editor, he could still write for the magazine.

As the '60s progressed, alcoholism took its toll on the McLaughlins' relationship and their health. By the end of the decade, the couple had separated, and Robert, after retiring from *Time* in 1968, moved to Florida. Mike was rumored to have had a long affair with one of her therapists. Robert died of cirrhosis of the liver and heart failure on October 23, 1973, age 65, in Coral Gables. Mike then moved into her husband's condo, resigning from *Glamour*, where she had been an editor for nearly a dozen years. She died in Coral Gables of lung cancer on December 20, 1983.

❦

Inevitably, McLaughlin reveals herself in her aphorisms far more deftly than any posthumous characterization based on public records and conversations and email exchanges with those who knew her. Even more than with most collections, the *Neurotic's Notebooks* are an autobiography in epigrams. This is partly because the *mots* are not all, strictly speaking, aphorisms (see below). Some are simply wry observations about herself. But from the aphorisms themselves, readers will undoubtedly infer things about McLaughlin's relationship with her mother ("A woman who didn't love her mother will never quite believe that her children love her."), her husband ("After the chills and fever of love, how nice is the 98.6 degrees of marriage!" "A first-rate marriage is like a first-rate hotel: expensive, but worth it.") and children ("One of life's few really reliable pleasures: to have a family you love, and to leave them for a week."), and her feelings about her calling ("Everybody can write; writers can't do anything else.") and her career. ("Failure can get to be a rather comfortable old friend." "My bootstraps have taken me the usual distance.")

While there have been a few aphorists with sunny personalities—Goethe, Franklin—most are a pretty mordant lot, and McLaughlin is no exception:

No one really listens to anyone else, and if you try it for a while, you'll see why.

From time to time we encounter people of a cheerful, kindly, unenvious nature. They usually run elevators.

We long for self-confidence, till we look at the people who have it.

She had a lot of inconsequential things to do; that is, she was happy.

We all have a pretty clear understanding of goodness, but it seldom applies to the situation we're in at the moment.

The know-nothings are, unfortunately, seldom the do-nothings.

Beauty often fades, but seldom so swiftly as the joy it gives.

A generous woman, a man with empathy, a cabdriver who keeps his mouth shut: these almost do not exist.

The head never rules the heart, but just becomes its partner in crime.

When anyone gets the fate he deserves, it's quite coincidental.

People are like birds: on the wing, all beautiful; up close, all beady little eyes.

A full list of McLaughlin's cynical observations would take pages, of course. But "pessimism," she reminds us, "is as silly as optimism," just "less destructive." And though she had a temper ("I once lamented my bad temper to a doctor, and he said of his own: I accept it, like a withered arm."), she was anything but an angry and resentful person, either in the recollections of those who knew her, or in her quips. Bitterness is always leavened by wit.

Any number of her aphorisms could serve as an epitaph, but this might be appropriate:

Tough and funny and little bit kind: that is as near to perfection as a human being can be.

❧

The aphorism is a curious hybrid. On the one hand, it is usually a pithy generalization about human nature, or about the behavior of some subset of humanity—a sort of psychological or sociological haiku. On the other hand, it reveals more about the character of the writer than any other genre, even including the essay.

A subset of humanity usually not anatomized is "the neurotic," a clan of which McLaughlin regards herself as a member in good standing. The term no longer has the currency it did in the '40s, '50s, and '60s, of course, when nearly everyone who lived in Manhattan was in analysis, or had friends, relatives, and colleagues who were. But this hardly means the anxieties, depressions, and compulsions of what was once called the neurotic personality have disappeared, vanquished by Prozac and other antidepressants, or cured by the smorgasbord of New Age therapies not on offer in the '50s. Readers not on medications or seeing therapists will still wince at some of her shafts. There is no point in further defining the term "neurotic," as McLaughlin does so repeatedly and, sometimes, brilliantly. ("Neurotics are sure that no one understands them, and they wouldn't have it any other way.") Another editor may have assigned the definitions of the neurotic to a section of their own, but McLaughlin clearly wanted them dispersed throughout the books.

A note on the selection: No aphorism has been excluded because it is "politically incorrect." A handful, however, with references that are dated, have been omitted, as have a few that seemed neither original, true, nor amusing.

"To be an only child is to have a very unreliable companion."

Mignon in New York,
about 4 years old.

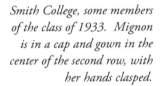

Smith College, some members of the class of 1933. Mignon is in a cap and gown in the center of the second row, with her hands clasped.

"How strange that the young should always think the world is against them—when in fact that is the only time it is for them."

Mignon Audrey Bushel,
in the yearbook for the class of 1933.

Youthful Poet

"*Everybody can write; writers can't do anything else.*"
The "youthful poet" and features writer for *The New York American*, 1935.

"*Being Irish is, no matter how real, a pose.*"
Lieutenant McLaughlin, 1945.

"*A successful marriage requires falling in love many times, always with the same person.*"
Robert and Mignon in 1944, in a picture taken for *Vogue* by Gretchen van Tassel.

"*We live for our children, but only as our parents lived for us: ready to make all the wrong sacrifices.*"
The McLaughlin family, Newburyport, Massachusetts, 1947.
Thomas, 3, is sitting on his father's lap, and James, 2, on his mother's.

"Charm makes everyone feel wonderful except, often, its possessor."
Mignon, Fair Harbor, Fire Island, 1967

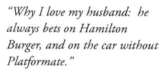

"Why I love my husband: he always bets on Hamilton Burger, and on the car without Platformate."
Robert, 1961

"A critic can only review the book he has read, not the one which the writer wrote."
Mignon, mid-1960s.

APERÇUS

1. Love and Marriage

No one has ever loved anyone the way everyone wants to be loved.

In many marriages, one partner can't flirt and the other can't not.

It seems unfair, but the taxes are higher on a small love than on a great one.

Love, like money, is offered most freely to those in least need of it.

When we have been humiliated by someone we love, it takes all our strength to pretend to recover from it.

Men never know how tired they are till their wives sit them down for a nice long talk.

It is a feeling at once stimulating and flat, to know that someone you do not love is in love with you.

"If I should die, would you marry again?" Women always ask this question of their husbands, and then wonder which is the more insulting answer: "Yes," or "Certainly not."

What we love about love is the fever, which marriage puts to bed and cures.

Love looks forward, hate looks back, and anxiety has eyes all over its head.

How can a man marry wisely in his twenties? The girl he's going to wind up wanting hasn't even been born.

Whether a marriage survives its crises depends on who's around when they happen.

When we get over a love, we remember one or two of its high moments, and all of its low ones.

The office marriage is easier to arrange than the office divorce.

Love is the silent saying and saying of a single name.

After the chills and fever of love, how nice is the 98.6 degrees of marriage!

When we discuss those we love with those who do not love them, the end of love is near.

A woman can seldom bring herself to break off a love affair; she wants the man to do it, but on her own terms.

A woman wants her husband to stay by her side when she needs him at parties, and go away when she doesn't.

We are always baffled and annoyed by a happy marriage between two people we dislike.

If you made a list of the reasons why any couple got married, and another list of the reasons for their divorce, you'd have a hell of a lot of overlapping.

No one can understand love who has not experienced infatuation. And no one can understand infatuation, no matter how many times he has experienced it.

A woman ought to look up to her husband, if only a half-inch.

Insult, not flattery, is the great aphrodisiac.

When we first fall in love, we feel that we know all there is to know about life, and perhaps we are right.

When desire has been satisfied, we can begin to think seriously about love.

Pity all newlyweds. She cooks something nice for him, and he brings her flowers, and they kiss and think: How easy marriage is.

If their husbands died, most middle-aged women would immediately look ten years younger.

If you think you must find someone worthy of your love, you never will.

Desire creates havoc when it is the only thing between two people, or when it is what's missing.

If he suddenly falls in love with someone else, a husband may not start wanting a divorce; but if he suddenly makes a lot of money, he usually will.

A perfect marriage is one in which "I'm sorry" is said just often enough.

We welcome passion, for the mind is briefly let off duty.

We lavish on animals the love we are afraid to show to people. They might not return it; or worse, they might.

Many wives are forgiven for falling; few, for falling ill.

Two who want only each other will always be wooed by the rest of the world.

"I am as I am" is another way of saying "I can do without your love."

We are irritated by rascals, intolerant of fools, and prepared to love the rest. But where are they?

We choose those we like; with those we love, we have no say in the matter.

The marriage of convenience has this to recommend it: we are better judges of convenience than we are of love.

Lust is the most defensible sin: it might have turned out to be love.

Boredom is often the cause of promiscuity, and always its result.

We all dream of being the darling of everybody's darling.

Says a well-known Broadway producer: when a man hires a new secretary, he should sleep with her at once; until he does, they won't get any work done.

A woman who had to be won from another man never lets her husband forget it.

A woman always dreams of love in terms of total commitment; the man's, that is.

He's in for trouble—the man whose wife is detested by all women and desired by all men.

For most of us, desire exceeds desirability, and long outlives it.

People we can't tease, we can't love.

She loves him if, even when she's not thinking about him, she's thinking about him.

Cocktail parties are an anachronism for those who already have the mates they want.

Many marriages are simply working partnerships between businessmen and housekeepers.

Beauty often fades, but seldom so swiftly as the joy it gives.

The excesses of love soon pass, but its insufficiencies torment us forever.

The hardest-learned lesson: that people have only their kind of love to give, not our kind.

⌘

Women are right about love: it's better than housework any day.

When love goes wrong, a man wants to walk out, and a woman to stay and cry.

Men marry sexy little girls for some other quality, as they never tire of telling you.

We all become great explorers during our first few days in a new city, or a new love affair.

Every wife who doesn't much love her husband considers it his fault.

Love is to men an embarrassment, even the word; it is to women an excuse for existence, especially the word.

A woman's convinced that love will last, a man that it won't; and you know which is more often surprised.

Lovers' quarrels end in kisses, each a little less innocent than the one before.

The more serious your love affair, the more people will find it ridiculous.

Hateful pretty women always get married, and so do an amazing number of hateful homely ones.

No sensible woman ever asks her husband whether or not to color her hair.

Naturally, the neurotic wants you to love him twice as much, for he's going to cut it in half anyway.

Two who embark on a love affair, both knowing it's not likely to last, deserve the worst they get—which is apt to be pretty bad.

If you habitually quarrel with the one you love, you might as well learn to enjoy it.

Marriage represents the intervention of the state in a love affair which probably wasn't going to end well anyway.

When a husband and wife agree all the time, he's henpecked.

People often say they love each other when they don't, but it's strange how often just saying it makes it come true.

Many quarrels are murmuringly resolved in bed. And many silently start there.

Affairs are just as disillusioning as marriage, and much less restful.

If you can't resolve a quarrel gracefully, don't get married.

Love requires a willingness to die; marriage a willingness to live.

If you keep falling in and out of love with others, you grow shallow. If they keep falling in and out of love with you, you grow brutalized.

When a man's wife and his mistress get cozy together, it's time for both of them—no, for all three of them— to move on.

Shrew: a woman who doesn't know her own strength till she finds her husband's weakness.

When a man stops being in love with you, it's no consolation to remind yourself that you may not have been in love with him in the first place.

A woman asks little of love: only that she be able to feel like a heroine.

Marriage is the refuge of the very lonely, and the very self-sufficient.

Long engagements make everyone nervous, and are therefore a good rehearsal for marriage.

The difference, in love, between normal people and neurotic ones: the neurotic sees more clearly the end of love coming, but is just as powerless to stop it.

Women completely plot the course of every love affair, and are completely wrong.

A woman's mink coat represents the sacrifice of a lot of little animals, including her husband.

Never cross-question your husband about what kept him so late; he might discover how easy it is to lie.

You will never again be so self-centered as in the midst of a selfless love affair.

A first-rate marriage is like a first-rate hotel: expensive, but worth it.

In the arithmetic of love, one plus one equals everything, and two minus one equals nothing.

A woman needs at least one man on whom to test her sense of power; he's the wrong man to marry, though.

Love fills a man's eyes with smiles, a woman's with tears.

Love is often gentle, desire always a rage.

How it rejoices a middle-aged woman when her husband criticizes a pretty girl!

Women insist upon marriage and then hate it; men are dragged there and then love it.

Reminder to clever wives: it's better to be kind than witty, and practically impossible to be both.

A man will desert the wife he loves more often than the type he loves.

There's no such thing as an innocent flirtation, only one which doesn't quite make it.

If you're really in love, you'll keep seeing him, even in crowds he's not in.

Of the few happy marriages a neurotic sees around him, most seem unsuitable.

You might as well withdraw love as threaten to withdraw it; to one who loves you, these are equal catastrophes.

Advice to women who remarry: never spell out to your second husband how much you loved, or hated, your first.

If marriage is your object, you'd better start by loving your subject.

Neurotics marry and tell themselves that things will change. It's like writing poetry on a typewriter: possible, but just barely.

At the beginning of a love affair, not even the neurotic is a neurotic.

"What's for dinner?" is the only question many husbands ask their wives, and the only one to which they care about the answer.

There are three iron links in the neurotic's chain: unloving, unlovable, and unloved.

No wife can forgive her husband for saying angry things to her and then placidly going to sleep.

A woman with a good husband, and sons, will flirt till the day she dies.

To the neurotic, each love affair seems like a curtain going up for the first time, each quarrel like a curtain going down forever.

A successful marriage requires falling in love many times, always with the same person.

A man will overlook much in his wife, if she just doesn't keep him waiting.

With the neurotic, it's never too late for someone to love him—only too late to do him any good.

A husband only worries about a particular Other Man; a wife distrusts her whole species.

Love unlocks doors and opens windows that weren't even there before.

All love is probationary, a fact which frightens women and exhilarates men.

Some marriages break up and some do not, and in our world you can usually explain the former better than the latter.

Separate rooms are a luxury no happily married couple can afford.

2. Home and Children

If you had an unhappy childhood, you will always want to sleep late in the morning.

Your children are neither as bad nor as good as you imagine. But then, neither are you.

Middle-class families are smaller than they used to be, but there is still not enough love to go around.

Small children are always boiling or freezing or starving.

It would be kinder to murder the ugly children of beautiful parents. Life will, anyway.

We start out determined to see that our children are good; we soon settle for having them nice.

Home is a place you can leave whenever you like, but they can't put you out.

The children of flamboyant parents usually have twice their taste, and half their style.

Every American child should grow up knowing a second language, preferably English.

In any family, measles are less contagious than bad habits.

I am a splendid daughter to the parents of my friends.

A childhood can be judged sheltered or not according to which was learned first, the four-letter word or the euphemism.

The only mothers it is safe to forget on Mother's Day are the good ones.

To be an only child is to have a very unreliable playmate.

Expensive hotels are as full as state institutions of old ladies whose children don't want them around—even with all their money.

There are children born to be children, and others who must mark time till they can take their natural places as adults.

Even in the same family, one child will always instinctively know when to ask for things, and another won't.

We tell our children things which we know are not so, but which we wish were so.

A child born suspicious will rummage around in a box of identical candies.

I like it at Klein's, and the automat; and at Harry's Bar, and the Met. I'm depressed by the middle-class places, where I suppose I belong. But then, it's always been so: neurotics are seldom at home at home.

It must infuriate our children to see us always so much more forbearing with everybody else's.

One of life's few really reliable pleasures: to have a family you love, and to leave them for a week.

They generally give the least to their children who give the most to their friends.

Learning too soon our limitations, we never learn our powers.

We live for our children, but only as our parents lived for us: ready to make all the wrong sacrifices.

Children expect to eat when they're hungry; our job is to teach them to eat when there's food.

Fat grown-ups may be jolly, but fat children stare at you malevolently in every public place.

When you refuse to explain something to a child on the theory that he would not understand, you're probably right, and it's probably unsavory.

Hot dogs always seem better out than at home; so do French-fried potatoes; so do your children.

We see our children doing only middling well among their contemporaries, and we shudder to think of them out in the great world.

The parents of private-school children are generally over-eager and over-aged.

If you can see in your children most of your own faults, you have failed as a parent, but succeeded as a neurotic.

The repetitions of family life provide most of its charm, and its horror.

The grimmest memory of childhood: being told to Go Out and Play.

It's unnerving to find out whom your children most admire.

Our children know we lie to them, but not—thank God—how much.

A simple pun is the lowest common denominator between children's speech and adults'.

Good mothers, like bad ones, sometimes holler and slap. But the children aren't fooled.

A happy childhood is the best horseshoe nail.

Children lack morality, but they also lack fake morality.

The family unit is man's noblest device for being bored.

The fault no child loses is the one he was most punished for.

✑

It's easy enough to get along with a loved and loving child—at least until you try to get him to do something.

There's one desirable place to be long-winded: in letters back home.

One woman will brag about her children, while another complains about hers; they could probably swap children without swapping tunes.

The way to find out about daughters: have sons

If your child doesn't think you're wonderful, you certainly aren't.

There is no way to repay a mother's love, or lack of it.

That home is happy where the refrigerator cleans itself.

There's an awful lot of blood around that water is thicker than.

No matter how many Christmas presents you give your child, there's always that terrible moment when he's opened the very last one. That's when he expects you to say, "Oh yes, I almost forgot," and take him out and show him the pony.

Suburb: a place that isn't city, isn't country, and isn't tolerable.

In adolescence, our children's complexions erupt, and so do their feelings. Our inadequate prescription for both: frequent cold showers.

Likely as not, the child you can do the least with will do the most to make you proud.

Ma-ma does everything for the baby, who responds by saying Da-da first.

Best neurotic way to show your children you regard them as grown-ups: quarrel fiercely with them.

I hope that when the time comes, I'll be a good mother-in-law. I have only one qualification for it: I always love the girls who love my sons.

Never let your children be greater snobs than you are.

A woman who didn't love her mother will never quite believe that her children love her.

Your children vividly remember every unkind thing you ever did to them, plus a few you really didn't.

Setting up headquarters for your teenaged children and their friends? Make it Liberty Hall, a mile or so this side of Licenseville.

We don't mind our children having different virtues from ours, but it seems disloyal of them to have different faults.

A happy child is a great testimonial to his parents, but only if they think he did it all himself.

A parent who has never apologized to his children is a monster. If he's always apologizing, his children are monsters.

A marriage without children is like a Chinese dinner without rice: the flavor may be there, but not the substance.

Families who hate each other seem almost glued together; a happy home is such a free place that there is seldom anyone in it.

I used to worry that I'd have fat children who'd glare at me and say "Oh, Mother!" Instead I have thin children who glare at me and say "Oh, Mother!"

The little of my childhood that I can remember is the part I still play out today.

Always plan on a traditional family Christmas dinner, and a traditional family fight afterward.

The neurotic—anywhere he hangs himself is home.

Children are the noisiest creatures on earth, but they never forgive a mother who screams at them.

If your children spend most of their time in other people's houses, you're lucky; if they all congregate in your house, you're blessed.

The ideal home: big enough for you to hear the children, but not very well.

Daddy asks his daughter "Whose little girl are you?", and Mommy has her first twinge of jealousy.

Nobody has a happy childhood, said a young man who was the happiest child I ever knew.

Your children tell you casually years later what it would have killed you with worry to have known at the time.

3. Men and Women

Men will make all sorts of allowances for a pretty woman, and women for an unmarried man.

We are always surprised to see girl babies behaving like girls from the very start, and boys like boys; we seem to imagine that we had to learn it.

A noble old man deserves to be listened to, whether he attributes his longevity to yogurt, cigars, hard work, or God.

Women flirt to keep their stock high, men to get somewhere.

Women go to beauty parlors for the unmussed look men hate.

No good neurotic finds it difficult to be both opinionated and indecisive.

A man wants a woman who can still surprise him, but only when he's in the mood for it.

Men prefer brief praise, pitched high; women are satisfied with praise in a lower key, just so it goes on and on.

Desire is in men a hunger, in women only an appetite.

Women are the right age for just a few years; men, for most of their lives.

A woman who lets herself go wants to die.

When women feel they have learned to forgive their mothers—and men, their fathers—all it usually means is that they've decided to allow themselves the same kind of behavior.

An attractive woman likes feminine company until she's twenty, and after she's thirty-five.

Others follow patterns; we alone are unpredictable.

A young woman can live off the folly of men; a man of any age can live off the folly of women.

Most women have their next husbands picked out, and the next, if necessary.

A man looks for mistresses, a woman for husbands; the wonder is that they ever get together.

A woman can tell you exactly what she was wearing during every crisis in her life.

No woman ever breaks off an affair simply because it's unsuitable.

A man who once in awhile says something nice is like a woman who once in a while makes up her eyes: it's becoming, but rather startling.

When a woman's tongue stops, her thoughts begin.

When men complain that they don't understand women, they mean that they don't want to be bothered trying.

Most clubwomen are not fools; they know they would be objects of derision even if they didn't belong to a club.

With women, the urge to heal is seldom more than a step ahead of the urge to wound.

Naturally women gossip: what's the use of knowing it first if you can't tell it first?

I hate being so intolerant, and I wouldn't be if people didn't deserve it.

Women have plenty of early foot; too bad it's a distance race.

Nymphomaniac: a woman as obsessed with sex as an average man.

The proud man can learn humility, but he will be proud of it.

A silent servant is theoretically desirable, but will drive most women crazy.

Women do not live longer than men; they only exist longer.

We can never understand other people's motives, nor their furniture.

"I learn from my mistakes," we say proudly, backing off the cliff.

It upsets women to be, or not to be, stared at hungrily.

Men talk better than women, work better, think better. But women love better, feel more deeply, and keep the arena tidy.

The neurotic would like to trust his analyst—if only because he's paying him so much money. But he can't—because if the analyst really cared, he'd be doing it for nothing.

When a woman reaches forty, she must wait twenty years for her husband to catch up.

Years of observation have convinced me that a man's attitude towards dogs and cats tells you nothing about his character.

Girlishness suits no women, and very few girls.

Everyone wants to feel wanted, but not for dangerous missions.

Most women would like to dress imaginatively, but they glare at any woman who does.

The total history of almost anyone would shock almost everyone.

Women polish the silver and water the plants and wait to be really needed.

Being Irish is, no matter how real, a pose.

It makes us melancholy, and should, that we cannot say the things which people so desperately want to hear.

Frigidity is the great American disease: a physical thing with women, an emotional thing with men.

Against all reason, women thrill to the sound of a ringing phone.

It has always upset decent people to see others having to do what they would not want to have to do themselves.

On stage and off, we care what happens to a beautiful woman, whether she can act or not.

Behind every hot-blooded man there's some woman patiently waiting for him to cool down.

There are very few single-minded people in the world, and even fewer who can resist them.

There are always a few people you do a lot for, and a few who do a lot for you, but they're not the same people.

Spite is never lonely; envy always tags along.

A man who lives by bilking women gives them first what they live for: wonderful preliminaries.

The neurotic never fears those who hate him—except when they say they love him.

A virtuous woman is perpetually threatened by a cloud no bigger than a man's hand.

Women are good listeners, but it's a waste of time telling your troubles to a man unless there's something specific you want him to do.

The mark of the neurotic: to imagine that you're the only one who cares deeply about anything.

Among the French, the Italians, the Jews, there is a sort of racial obsession with fruit.

A woman always knows when it's her husband you like, not herself.

Even cowards can endure hardship; only the brave can endure suspense.

Try as we will, we cannot honestly recall our youth, for we have lost the feel of its main ingredient: suspense.

It's always safe to tell people they're looking wonderful.

Women gather together to wear silly hats, eat dainty food, and forget how unresponsive their husbands are. Men gather to talk sports, eat heavy food, and forget how demanding their wives are. Only where children gather is there any real chance of fun.

People who won't have a TV set in their house get more pleasure from their refusal than most of us get from TV.

He who shows you his weakness today will show you his brutality tomorrow.

We come late, if at all, to wine and philosophy: whiskey and action are easier.

Men feel that women somehow drag them down, and women feel that way about men. It's possible that both are right.

The trouble with women is men; the trouble with men, men.

The first two days of a vacation are endless; then it flies.

We work for praise, and dawdle once we have it.

Most of us will gladly watch old movies sooner than think old thoughts.

On earth's last morning, children will play, women will putter, men will compromise.

The despair of mankind makes no sense to a cheerful competent woman.

∞

Men are convinced that women have it easy, but they haven't convinced many women.

Men gossip less than women, but mean it.

There's no one so ruthless as a timid woman striking back.

The way to a man's heart is through his stomach, especially if you tell him how flat it is.

Trust a woman, and not a man, in causal moments; a man, and not a woman, in crucial ones. For that's when each tends to tell the truth.

Shopping brings out gluttony in a woman, impatience in a man.

Ask a woman why she's so happy, and she'll immediately wonder if she is.

The woman just ahead of you at the supermarket checkout has all the delectable groceries you didn't even know they carried.

She was a real pet: both dogged and catty.

Women let you know how awful they feel, and how bravely they're concealing it.

Women who feel naked without their lipstick are well over thirty.

No one really listens to anyone else, and if you try it for a while you'll see why.

A man will do anything to win a certain woman; afterwards, he thinks he must have been crazy.

Good-looking girls break hearts, and goodhearted girls mend them.

No woman wants to see herself too clearly.

Many beautiful women have been made happy by their own beauty, but no intelligent woman has ever been made happy by her own intelligence.

Men who wear glasses forever make passes.

Many a quarrel has been deferred by a woman's tears— but not for long.

Man: a creature who runs out of money even faster than he runs out of love.

When a man falls in love, he wants to go to bed. When a woman falls in love, she wants to talk about it.

"If I've told you once, I've told you a thousand times." That's every woman's autobiography.

Jewelry seldom excites the beholder, but it certainly makes the wearer feel beautiful.

The average woman's a success if she pleases one man; the great beauty's a failure if one man gets away.

Nothing brings out the gallantry in a man like his daughter's pretty friends.

The meekest woman is merely a Becky Sharp whose nerve has failed her.

Men want a woman both sexy and lady-like, women want a man at once rough and tender. Isn't it wonderful when both imagine themselves satisfied?

Women are invariably at their most beautiful when with men they care nothing about.

Few women care what a man looks like, and a good thing too.

By the time women are kind to each other, they're no longer rivals.

No matter what she looks like, every woman secretly considers herself rather seductive.

It's the nature of some women to wait for the man who wants them, of others to go after the man they want; it's important for every woman to decide which type she is.

Women are appalled by men's recklessness; men are reassured by women's lack of it.

A woman will do anything to keep a pretty figure, but hardly anything to get one.

Men really prefer reasonably attractive women; they go after the sensational ones to impress other men.

A woman will wear her heart on her sleeve, if she thinks it goes with her dress.

A woman on a diet soon feels like Joan of Arc.

If a woman can get a man to talk to her about himself, she can get him to propose. Especially if he's unmarried at the time.

It's wonderful to watch pretty women with character grow beautiful.

Sarcasm, like haemophilia, is transmitted by the females of the family.

With men, as with women, the main struggle is between vanity and comfort; but with men, comfort often wins.

Women's chatter bores men, but not half so much as it bores women.

Women simultaneously adore and suspect any bachelor over thirty.

Women are never landlocked: they're always mere minutes away from the briny deep of tears.

Men enjoy being thought of as hunters, but are generally too lazy to hunt. Women, on the other hand, love to hunt but would rather nobody knew it.

Men who don't like girls with brains don't like girls.

Women talk and talk, but men hear only the self-incriminating things.

With two people who can really talk to each other, sex is no more than a marvelous bonus. And vice versa.

Fortunately, not everyone who could kill you does.

Women claim to be intuitive, but they're always stunned.

Every man is unique whose wife makes him feel so.

In every roué, there's a bit of Peter Pan—impervious, though, to the Wendy in the woman.

Hate leaves ugly scars, love leaves beautiful ones.

Some women love only what they can hold in their arms; others, only what they can't.

Ask a woman how she feels and she tells you. Ask a lady, and she says, "Fine, thank you."

If you must reread old love letters, better pick a room without mirrors.

4. Health, Happiness, Self-Esteem

"Pull yourself together" is seldom said to anyone who can.

Humiliation is a vast country of imprecise boundaries. If you think you're there, you are. The neurotic's rule: when in doubt, go ahead and feel humiliated.

Nobody wants constructive criticism; it's all we can do to put up with constructive praise.

Tragedy isn't getting something, or failing to get it; it's losing something you already have.

The moment we're born they try to make us cry, and it sometimes seems as though they never stop.

After he has had his tantrum, the neurotic expects those around him to feel friendly and relaxed; after all, he does.

Make a habit of telling the truth, or make a habit of lying: to decide each case on its own merits is exhausting, and hardly ever worth it.

The more aggressions you get rid of, the more there are that you cannot get rid of.

The fault we admit to is seldom the fault we have, but it has a certain relationship to it, a somewhat similar shape, like that of a sleeve to an arm.

You will turn over many a futile new leaf till you learn we must all write on scratched-out pages.

Irrelevant things may happen to you, but once they have happened, they all become relevant.

It does not undo harm to acknowledge that we have done it; but it undoes us not to acknowledge it.

Guilt is the neurotic's feather: he uses it now to slap his own wrist, now to tickle his own throat.

Ideals are at us like nagging wives, always tormenting us for our own good.

If you can tell anyone about it, it's not the worst thing you ever did.

A new wound makes the old ones ache again.

Courage can't see around corners, but goes around them anyway.

The neurotic despises his own behavior, but thinks even less of yours.

When the pain is great enough, we will let anyone be doctor.

What you can't get out of, get into wholeheartedly.

We are never more self-righteous than when giving up what we should have shunned all along.

Some are born knowing how to charm the birds off the trees; no one has ever learned it.

Vanity is absolute: some of us can swallow any compliment, the rest can swallow none.

Motto for the self-indulgent: *Je ne me refuse rien.*

Reason tells us that money will not buy happiness; passion says it will. Reason tell us virtue is its own reward; passion demands more. Reason tells us passion will be our undoing; passion replies that reason is cold and dead. Both seem to speak the truth, so we listen to both, and remain neurotic.

The thrill, when you first leave a middle-class home: not having to eat a good hot meal.

The neurotic's strongest fantasy is that he has no fantasies. The real is very real to him, the unreal even more so.

"Grow up!" we tell others, calmly sucking our thumb.

If the battles you care about have been lost, it's a hollow victory to have won the war.

During his moments of happiness, the neurotic always feels—in the teeth of evidence—that that is his normal state.

From time to time we encounter people of a cheerful, kindly, unenvious nature. They usually run elevators.

I once lamented my bad temper to a doctor, and he said of his own: I accept it, like a withered arm.

Neurosis is no worse than a bad cold; you ache all over, and it's made you a mess, but you won't die from it.

The chief reason for drinking is the desire to behave in a certain way, and to be able to blame the alcohol.

No compliment could be paid us which we didn't in some part merit; no insult, either.

Goods are displayed by thousands of shopkeepers with a sense of beauty that finds no other outlet.

Neurotics believe in happiness, but as in the old joke: You can't get there from here.

The best work is done with the heart breaking, or overflowing.

If you have to do it every day, for God's sake do it well.

We long for self-confidence, till we look at the people who have it.

Every day of our lives we are on the verge of making those slight changes that would make all the difference.

The neurotic circles ceaselessly above a fogged-in airport.

When hope is hungry, everything feeds it.

Slavishly we imitate; and slavishly, rebel.

At night, neurotics may toil not, but oh how they spin!

True remorse is never just a regret over consequence; it is a regret over motive.

Virtue is the safest medicine: non-toxic, and non-habit-forming.

She had a lot of inconsequential things to do; that is, she was happy.

Neurotics would like to sleep all the time, and to be awakened only when there is good news.

To one who persistently belittles your achievements, it is only sensible to exaggerate them: with luck, you come out even.

Pessimism is as silly as optimism, but less destructive.

The handicapped are not a special group, but only the ones on whom it shows.

The neurotic wants to be alone—but he wants to be alone with someone else.

Self-confidence grows on trees, in other people's orchards.

We always forgive ourselves for the wrong things: for what we could have helped, instead of what we couldn't.

Self-discipline is the hardest thing to learn; you need self-discipline to learn it.

If despair will yield at all, it will yield to a good night's sleep.

We often pray to be better, when in truth we only want to feel better.

Revenge leads to an empty fullness, like eating dirt.

It's axiomatic, in geometry, that a thing is always equal to itself. But any neurotic can tell you better, for he is not.

Courage alone can tell you the right moment for resignation.

I do not trust those who are above name-dropping. The suppression of small vices always exacts too high a toll.

Neurotics live as animals eat: gobble or go without

Sloth: a state in which you envy those who are busy, but despise what they're busy at. Spiritual sloth, or acedia, was known as The Sin of the Middle Ages. It's the sin of my middle age, too.

When "Why not do it?" barely outweighs "Why do it?"—don't do it.

Popular people always think it's silly: all this talk about goodness.

If the pain wanders, do not waste your time with doctors.

"Life is meant to be lived." Telling that to most of us is as useful as telling a mouse that aluminum is meant to be made into cars.

I'm afraid to win, and afraid to lose; I hate a draw and can't stop competing; otherwise I'm fine.

My bootstraps have taken me the usual distance.

We listen only to those who flatter, amuse, or comfort us, and you know that's not many people.

The neurotic is always leaning on somebody who is already leaning on somebody else.

❦

Nobody knows the trouble we've seen—but we keep trying to tell them.

Neurotics dream of a good life, or a great suicide note.

Ours is not the only story, just the most interesting one.

The neurotic feels as though trapped in a gas-filled room where at any moment someone, probably himself, will strike a match.

They threaten me with lung cancer, and still I smoke and smoke. If they'd only threaten me with hard work, I might stop.

Don't be yourself—be someone a little nicer.

Neurotics deal with anxiety by clinging to half a rope halfway down a well.

The only patience the neurotic knows is that to be found in a bottle of sleeping pills.

Most of us are pretty good at postponing our nervous breakdowns till we can afford them.

For the happiest life, rigorously plan your days, and leave your nights open to chance.

As every woman knows, laugh and the world laughs with you; cry and some man will comfort you.

Offices are full of people who are only alive from Monday to Friday.

Our protestations don't often fool others, but they still serve a purpose: they fool us.

Go on a diet, quit smoking, give up alcohol—but not all at once.

If you are neurotic and wish to hide it, go easy on coffee, pills, cigarettes, and alcohol—and keep your mouth shut.

A cynic is one who believes it matters not whether you win, nor how you play the game.

Neurotics always feel as though they were going way up or way down, which is odd in people going sideways.

I can't figure out why, but hangovers always make me terribly courteous.

The neurotic usually obeys his own Golden Rule: Hate they neighbor as thyself.

Grasp your opportunities, no matter how poor your health; nothing is worse for your health than boredom.

You can't truthfully explain your smallest action without fully revealing your character.

There's nothing wrong with most men's egos that the kowtowing of a headwaiter can't cure.

We're all loveable. At least in our own eyes. At least if you catch us at the right moment.

If you hate your lot but wouldn't trade it, it's not your lot that you hate.

A sense of humor is a major defense against minor troubles.

A small cut on one of my fingertips keeps reopening, and it's a brand-new thrill: seeing your own blood on the typewriter keys.

Without sex, alcohol, sleeping pills, you are always with yourself.

Nothing so rousingly raises your spirits as emerging from a gloomy movie into a sunny afternoon.

Neurotics are always looking for something new to overdo.

Charm makes everyone feel wonderful except, often, its possessor.

People who make the best of a bad bargain automatically have the beginnings of a good one.

A hypochondriac is one who has a pill for everything except what ails him.

Speak up when's time to, whether it's your turn or not.

Character is what emerges from all the little things you were too busy to do yesterday, but did anyway.

Other people's truth may comfort us, but only our own persuades us.

Failure can get to be a rather comfortable old friend.

I've just posed for a portrait, and it's an experience I recommend: the one time in your life when you can do absolutely nothing, and feel virtuous about it.

Neurotic: someone who can go from the bottom to the top, and back again, without ever once touching the middle.

Love, at best, is joy; work, though, can be ecstasy.

The two things that make office life endurable: coffee breaks and falling in love.

Halfway through exciting work is halfway to heaven.

Convinced that you're not ungrateful to others but they are to you? Congratulations; you're a true neurotic.

Acedia is not in every dictionary; just in every heart.

Tough and funny and little bit kind: that is as near to perfection as a human being can be.

Being neurotic is like shooting fish in a barrel, and missing them.

Neurotics are sure that no one understands them, and they wouldn't have it any other way.

It's terrifying to see someone inside of whom a vital spring seems to have broken. It's particularly terrifying to see him in your mirror.

There's no such thing as a humdrum life; to the person living it, it's all peaks and abysses.

Of course no one is as sensitive as you, but try to remember that they think they are.

If you find yourself a bit ridiculous, you can scarcely expect to be able to take anyone else very seriously.

The neurotic has no solid opinion as to how good or bad he is, so he constantly solicits the opinion of others, which he then rejects as too good or bad.

Some people never get hooked on anything, but among those who do, it's never just one thing.

When we say "If I don't do it, someone else will," we mean, of course, some other son of a bitch.

The only courage that matters is the kind that gets you from one moment to the next.

Neurotics are anxiety prone, accident prone, and often just prone.

5. The General Orneriness of Things

Not for nothing does the neurotic suffer—but not for anything very much, either.

If an article is attractive, or useful, or inexpensive, they'll stop making it tomorrow; if it's all three, they stopped making it yesterday.

Altruism is a hard master; but so is opportunism.

We can always show we don't care when we really don't; but that's not when we want to.

Each day we do what little we will of the little that we can.

Remember the fairy tale about the old man who was granted three wishes? He inadvertently wished for a nice black pudding, and of course one appeared. His wife berated him and he lost his temper and shouted: "I wish the black pudding were on the end of your nose!" Then it took his last wish to get the pudding off her nose. This leads me to a Rule of Life: Be careful what you wish for, because you always get it—and it's always black pudding.

Every creature stalks some other, catches it, and is caught.

There are now electrical appliances with the main unit so sealed in that it cannot be got at for repair. There have always been human beings like that.

Anything one man can do well, a good team can botch.

If it came true, it wasn't much of a dream.

More people would be really good, or really bad, if they just knew how.

Many of us are equal to life's emergencies who cannot bear its day-after-day-ness.

We are seldom happy with what we now have, but would go to pieces if we lost any part of it.

We cough because we can't help it, but others do it on purpose.

Plus ça change, plus ça go downhill.

An old racetrack joke reminds you that your program contains all the winners' names. I stare at my typewriter keys with the same thought.

Hope is the feeling we have that the feeling we have is not permanent.

It's impossible to be loyal to your family, your friends, your country, and your principles, all at the same time.

If there is something you must do and you cannot do it, you cannot do anything else.

Once you become self-conscious, there is no end to it; once you start to doubt, there is no room for anything else.

We all have a pretty clear understanding of goodness,
but it seldom applies to the situation we're in at the
moment.

We hear only half of what is said to us, understand only
half of that, believe only half of that, and remember
only half of that.

We try to tell the truth and cannot; then when we're
not trying at all, we blurt it out.

Each generation must watch the next, throwing away
its golden opportunities.

Practically nothing can interrupt pain—but ecstasy
ceases at the lightest footstep.

I tell you this, and I tell you plain:
What you have done, you will do again;
You will bite your tongue, careful or not,
Upon the already-bitten spot.

I want what I want when I want it: that is to say, when
you don't want me to have it.

Quantity is a poor substitute for quality—but it's the
only one around.

I am always undone by the remorse of others. Fortunately, it doesn't come up very often.

As we're human, we can't do what we can't do; as we're neurotic, we can't do what we can.

The three horrors of modern life—talk without meaning, desire without love, work without satisfaction.

The neurotic feels like a Christmas shopper who keeps dropping his packages, and it's raining.

Says the rude child: "No, I won't do it." Says the courteous grown-up: "Yes, I won't do it."

As we grow older, our capacity for enjoyment shrinks, but not our appetite for it.

Many of us go through life feeling as an actor might feel who does not like his part, and does not believe in the play.

When intellectuals lower their standards, they always expect fanfare.

Most of us would gladly give up adolescent pleasures in favor of mature ones, if we could just figure out what they are.

The know-nothings are, unfortunately, seldom the do-nothings.

Oh what a tangled web we weave when we first practice to weave.

From a wretched deed there is sometimes a good outcome, making penance even more unlikely than usual.

What you have become is the price you paid to get what you used to want.

It is romantic to expect that things will get better, cynical to suppose that they will not, bestial not to care.

❧

Things are never so bad that they can't get worse. But they're sometimes so bad they can't get better.

Good food, good sex, good digestion, good sleep: to these basic animal pleasures, man has added nothing but the good cigarette.

If I knew what I was so anxious about, I wouldn't be so anxious.

There is no way to say "I love you" in English.

Your best work always seems to have been done by someone else.

If they dare to cross-examine you, you're ruined; the really strong, no one dares to cross-examine.

The way the neurotic sees it: bars on his door mean that he's locked in; bars on your door mean that he's locked out.

Love gives no warning and no quarter; it is sneaky and cruel; if we weren't so lonely, we'd never put up with it.

Most of us become parents long before we have stopped being children.

Youth is not enough. And love is not enough. And success is not enough. And, if we could achieve it, enough would not be enough.

If you are brave too often, people will come to expect it of you.

Life is a mixed blessing, which we vainly try to unmix.

You can trust a sentimental person, every time, to be merciless.

Every martyr comes with a built-in bully.

A generous woman, a man with empathy, a cabdriver who keeps his mouth shut: these almost do not exist.

The head never rules the heart, but just becomes its partner in crime.

"Let your conscience be your guide" is a silly thing to say to a good man, or a bad one.

Fields can lie fallow, but we can't; we have less time.

Strong cruel women generally marry weak cruel men.

Sisyphus is the only one for whom it was a myth.

Scarves are often nice, but the only reason you get them for presents is that someone didn't know your size.

The best people seldom give you the best advice.

The trouble with ingénues: by the time a pretty young girl learns anything about acting, she's no longer a pretty young girl.

With each passing year, one has less to say, and knows better how to say it.

You know how you hate being interrupted, so why are you always doing it to me?

I know a man who married a woman he didn't love, because he thought that everyone else did. They still do, and he still doesn't.

Sensible reason to cheat at solitaire: you want something to turn out right, just once.

When you're about to issue that well-deserved ultimatum, just stop for a moment and remember the last time.

There have been cases of couples getting married who first met on a blind date—but your chances of winning the Irish Sweepstakes are slightly better.

Live and let live: now there's a pair of impossible commands!

Neurotics chase after people and jobs they don't really want, just to prove that they're like everybody else—which is the last thing they really want.

We always prefer war on our own terms to peace on someone else's.

The time we can often do something wonderful is when we are supposed to be doing something else.

When you're nervous it makes you cranky, and when you're cranky it makes people hostile, and when people are hostile it makes you nervous.

When anyone gets the fate he deserves, it's quite coincidental.

This morning, our twenty-year-old son enlisted in the Naval Air Reserve. You wait and wait for something to happen; then that's the sort of thing that happens.

The only totally benign inventions of our times: Kleenex, and the electric percolator.

We semaphore from ship to ship, but they're sinking, too.

People find it hard to be both comic and serious, though life manages it easily enough.

Few men have ever been able to resist doing the things that bring out the shrew in a woman.

People are like birds: on the wing, all beautiful; up close, all beady little eyes.

Most of us would rather risk catastrophe than read the directions.

There are different clothes in everyone's closet, but always the same old skeletons.

Most of us can easily do two things at once; what's all but impossible is to do one thing at once.

The time to begin most things is ten years ago.

6. Friends and Enemies

The neurotic always believes that his enemies are more sincere than his friends—and more sensible.

Every group feels strong once it has found a scapegoat.

We are keenly aware of the faults of our friends, but if they like us enough it doesn't matter.

It pains us more to hear praise of an enemy than criticism of a friend.

Our friends are seldom capable of telling us any profound truths about ourselves, and if they were, we would not be capable of listening.

Divided loyalties make you feel miserable, but important.

Every group of six or more has its inner circle, its outer circle, and its hangers-on.

Nothing so depresses us as a slow evening with people we like.

We are always apologizing to some of our friends for some of our other friends.

Most of us would try to be noble, if we just had a claque we could depend on.

We waste a lot of time running after people we could have caught by just standing still.

It is hard to forgive the kind of vacuous good looks which remind us of those who were more popular than we were at school.

Anyone you understand you can live without.

What we forgive too freely doesn't stay forgiven.

Bored with your present enemies? Make new ones! Tell two of your women friends that they look alike.

By the time you have lined up the third person on your side, the first two will have wandered off somewhere.

Finest single example of a neurotic remark: Oscar Levant's "I always hate them till they say hello."

The innocent bystander is a villain: he should have come in on our side.

It is important to our friends to believe that we are unreservedly frank with them, and important to the friendship that we are not.

For pleasure, chose the right friends; for pride, the right enemies.

Neurotic quarrels have always the same theme-song: Hate me and get it over with.

Friendship without malice is unimaginable.

There are people you can't give up till just once you've gained the advantage.

If some of the allies are shady, then so is some of the cause.

A big change in our own weight is more important than any friend's news.

A summer colony is a place where you work hard collecting dossiers on people who you don't care about.

What you cannot say to a friend's face, say very carefully behind his back.

The people you admire most you usually don't know very well.

We catch frightful glimpses of ourselves in the hostile eyes of others.

The faults you charge a friend with should never be more grievous than those which you admit to. "You're easily hurt." "You expect too much of yourself." "You're over-loyal." But no friend is worth it whom you must keep assuring: "Yes, you were absolutely right."

It is easy to apologize to those we haven't finished with.

Old friends soon exhaust the past if that is all they have in common.

When we meet someone who truly sees good in everyone, it is hard to believe that he knows the same people we do.

If you know of wounding things to say, sooner or later you'll say them.

You cannot trust people's descriptions of themselves, even when uncomplimentary.

There are truths too bitter to be told, but most of us have friends ready to tell them.

We care only about ourselves, and a handful of other attractive people.

The people for whom yesterday's friend always becomes today's enemy are the ones most recklessly eager to confide in today's friend.

The surest way to be hated is to be caught delivering the same compliment to two different people.

When a stranger identifies you from a friend's description, it's just as well you didn't hear the description.

∽

The neurotic keeps minute track of his enemies; it is only his friends he is careless about.

If people find your silences interesting, don't disillusion them.

No matter how many times you change jobs or mates or neighborhoods, there's always someone in your life you can't get along with.

When you're with people who have nothing to say, you're liable to say almost anything.

The neurotic never has friends: just enemies and potential enemies.

It takes charm to win over sulky people—charm and a willingness to waste your time.

Before you go, hope they remember you; before you return, hope they've forgotten.

Anyone can sit and talk all night, but it takes iron discipline to listen for fifteen minutes.

Nothing so blights a party as a hostess with plans for making it jolly.

Don't tell the neurotic your name or address or anything else irrelevant; all he wants to know is whether you're for him or against him.

The neurotic always wishes people would let him alone—until they do.

If no one will meet your eye, stop trying to tell your story.

There are people who hide their love from you, and people who hide their hate, and you'll be wise to stay away from both.

Coming across an old friend you haven't seen for years is like finding a forgotten suit in the back of the closet: you're glad to see it, but you soon discover it doesn't fit any more.

When humorless people laugh loudest and longest, it's a signal to the rest of us that they've had enough of our wit.

Every group has its favorite clown, and it's Rule One that he be unhappy.

Surrounded by people who love life, you love it too; surrounded by people who don't, you don't.

It's easier to part with a friend than an opinion.

To talk easily with people, you must firmly believe that either you or they are interesting. And even then it's not easy.

If a man likes his wife's best friend at all, he likes her too much.

People credit you with only half of what you have done—but blame you for only half, too.

Neurotics have plenty of non-neurotic friends, but not for long.

We never mind snobs who like us.

Those who are brutally honest are seldom so with themselves.

On converting an enemy into a friend, rejoice—but don't relax.

We're seldom drawn to a character we admire; only to a personality we like.

Duty seldom prompts us to tell people flattering things.

I'd like to be liked by everybody, because when people like me I usually like them, and I'd like to like everybody.

A friend: one who pretends he's as interested in your welfare as his own.

An enemy: one who has his own best welfare at heart, not yours.

An acquaintance: somebody you nod to if he nods first.

A bore: one who knows as well as you do what he is going to say next.

Friendships don't last long when they're used as wailing walls.

The neurotic lies awake at night, composing letters to those he hates. He seldom thinks of dropping a line to those he loves.

Neurotics would change places with anyone—except the people they know.

Never ask a hypochondriac how he is, nor a bore what he's been doing.

Every now and then you run across radiantly attractive people, and you're delighted to find they adore you, till you realize that they adore just about everybody—and that's what's made them radiantly attractive.

Heat blisters skin, and paint, and friendship.

If you started the rumor and it comes back to you substantially unchanged, you've got some mighty dull neighbors.

There are some people we just plain don't like the looks of, and they all nestle close to us at the beach.

7. Politics, Arts, Professions

Injure a businessman and he'll try to make you sorry; injure an artist and he'll try to make you immortal.

"It's wonderful to have you here," cries the TV host. "It's wonderful to be here," replies the TV guest. Now, if it were only wonderful for us watching.

Good plays require good audiences. In short: read them.

The jolliest men in America, for no reason I can see, are its grocery clerks.

Every society honors its live conformists and its dead troublemakers.

An artist usually has no friends except other artists, and usually they do not like his work.

Psychiatrists are terrible ads for themselves, like dermatologists with acne.

The first-rate mind is always curious, compassionate, original, and pessimistic.

In the theatre, as in life, we prefer a villain with a sense of humor to a hero without one.

It's awesome to realize that if your greatest potential talent is for riding a bicycle upside down on a high wire, you will somehow discover it.

Broadway audiences are dependably square. "Well, I'll be a son of a bitch" always gets a laugh; spoken by a little old lady, it brings down the house.

Stubborn, opinionated, self-righteous: there, I have drawn a character you've often met, but not in many American best-sellers.

Life's most painful condition: to be almost a celebrity.

Everybody can write; writers can't do anything else.

Theatre audiences can't be made to think and cry: at best, they can be made to think and laugh, or to feel and cry.

The two things I admire about actors: they can laugh when they're supposed to, and not laugh when they're not supposed to.

Belated obituary for Al Jolson: Only in America could a Jew make a million dollars pretending to be a Negro.

The tragedy of heroes is that they leave the right road; the tragedy for the rest of us is that we never find it at all.

A critic can only review the book he has read, not the one which the writer wrote.

There's nothing intrinsically wrong with lawyers, but there's something wrong with most lawyers.

The plague of governments is senile delinquency.

The Bohemian life is the same old difference, day after day.

Few of us write great novels; all of us live them.

No matter how brilliantly an idea is stated, we will not really be moved unless we have already half-thought of it ourselves.

Stay away from playwriting if you possibly can. That still leaves too many of us.

We have to call it "freedom": who'd want to die for "a lesser tyranny"?

⁓

My doctor is nice; every time I see him, I'm ashamed of what I think of doctors in general.

Politics makes strange bedfellows, but so do beds.

The chief function of an executive is to keep those who really do the work from doing it in peace.

The Liberal: conservatives see him as a dupe; radicals see him as a coward; even in his own eyes, he's no great bargain.

A subversive: one who doesn't like Walt Disney or Coca-Cola.

Neurotics make poor patriots; if you're ashamed of something as big as yourself, it's hard to be proud of something as small as your country.

If you really can't bear to do shabby things, forget about being an executive.

A recent survey was said to prove that the people we Americans most admire are our politicians and doctors. I don't believe it. They're simply the people we're most afraid of. And with the most reason.

In the hardware business, as in the theatre, the show must go on; it's just that the actors make a bigger fuss about it.

In medicine, no practitioner likes to charge another with malpractice. Among artists, it's the favorite pastime.

Few novels or plays could exist without at least one troublemaker in the group, and perhaps life couldn't either.

The greatest works of art and the vilest murders are motivated alike: to do one thing once that only you in all the world can do.

There's only one person who needs a glass of water oftener than a small child tucked in for the night, and that's a writer sitting down to write.

In Utopia, people will study art, and artists will study life.

Watch yourself on your first job; it's a perfect forecast of all jobs to come.

A doctor recently described to me "benign positional vertigo": it means you get dizzy in certain positions, but you can get over it without necessarily changing that position. Change "vertigo" to "anxiety" and you've summed up the neurotic's plight.

When a chef, a chemist, a tree surgeon talks about his work, we can all listen and learn; let an artist do it, though, and it just sounds pretentious.

Creative people usually head for the big cities: more than the theatres, museums, or libraries, they need each other.

Women vie with men for a lot of jobs that neither men nor women want.

To write the best possible play, start off with the best possible exposition scene, then go ahead and finish the play, then go back and lop off the exposition scene.

Nowhere but in the arts can talent, experience, dedication, and years of hard work lead to a steady decline in quality.

The artist and the housewife have this in common: though both can arbitrarily call it quits when they want to, neither can ever with certainty say: there is nothing more to be done.

It took man thousands of years to put words down on paper, and his lawyers still wish he wouldn't.

8. God and the Devil

I believe that of all the people in the world, only a certain tiny percentage is truly good; and I also believe that this percentage has remained mysteriously constant since the beginning of man.

They are driven to God by the least desirable path who have love to give and no one else to give it to.

When your cup runneth over, looketh out.

Many are saved from sin by being so inept at it.

Charity is a good way of reminding God that if we can do it, He can.

We wake in the night, to stereophonic silence.

God and the devil lose to a common enemy: inertia.

In any group of underprivileged children, there are some so ugly that we wonder at the cruelty of God.

Confession is good for the conscience, but it usually bypasses the soul.

Whatever we worship, short of God, is sure to be our undoing.

Despair is anger with no place to go.

According to Oscar Wilde, all that experience teaches us is that history repeats itself, and that the sin we do once and with loathing we will do many times and with pleasure. But the neurotic knows that the sin he does once and with loathing he will do many times and with loathing.

The most eloquent descriptions of virtue often come from those who do not possess it, and indeed they have the best vantage point for its appraisal.

In church, sacred music would make believers of us all—but preachers can be counted on to restore the balance.

The death of someone we know always reminds us that we are still alive—perhaps for some purpose which we ought to re-examine.

Comfort, or revelation: God owes us one of these, but surely not both.

A little embarrassment prevents a lot of goodness.

Those who turn to God for comfort may find comfort but I do not think they will find God.

God is less careful than General Motors, for He floods the world with factory rejects.

How tired God must be of guilt and loneliness, for that is all we ever bring Him.

We climb mountains because they are there, and worship God because he is not.

Without enthusiasm, virtue functions not at all, and vice only poorly.

When suffering comes, we yearn for some sign from God, forgetting we have just had one.

⌀

I dare to drink the water when there is reason to doubt, yet cannot make the same concession to God.

Minor vices lead to major ones, but minor virtues stay put.

Neurotics are afraid to pray: God might be listening.

Many cleaners give same-day service, which is more than most religions can promise you.

My religious position: I think that God could do a lot better, and I'm willing to give Him the chance.

Come Judgement Day, two groups alone will be saved: the cheerful, and the devout.

God doesn't measure his bounty, but oh how we do!

I half-believe in reincarnation, and I'd like to come back as an otter; so far as I know, it's impossible to be a bad otter.

A movement takes on strength when people are willing to die for it, but it doesn't necessarily take on virtue.

I know someone is who both evil and boring, which is surely a case of the devil doing God's work for Him.

If you lie all the time, you'll soon be the only one fooled by it.

I can't believe that God minds the disbelief of the young.

The neurotic believes that life has meaning, but his life hasn't.

If you truly believe in God, and the immortality of the soul, why do you get so mad when a malefactor goes unpunished.

I've been hiding from God, and I'm appalled to find how easy it is.

Basis for a workable religion: when you have nothing better to do, do something for someone else.

The young do not need God, and the old cannot find Him.

Most sermons sound to me like commercials—but I can't make out whether God is the Sponsor or the Product.

"Your money or your life." We know what to do when a burglar makes this demand of us, but not when God does.

Puritans will never believe it, but life is full of disagreeable things that aren't even good for you.

The neurotic's constant prayer: that nothing worse will happen.

If you take the high road and I take the low road, naturally I'll get there before you.

I often pray, though I'm not really sure Anyone's listening; and I phrase it carefully, just in case He's literary.

9. Getting and Spending

People keep telling us about their love affairs, when what we really want to know is how much money they make and how they manage on it.

We'd all like a reputation for generosity, and we'd all like to buy it on the cheap.

If everyone gave a tenth of his worldly goods to the person he most admired, the rich would get richer.

Life marks us down, so it's just as well that we start out by overpricing ourselves.

I am certain that nothing in life is wasted—unless, of course, everything is.

A good executive is one who makes people contentedly settle for less than they meant to get, in return for more than they meant to give.

Women usually love what they buy, yet hate two-thirds of what is in their closets.

The complexions of the rich seem not merely better than those of the poor, but as though made of some wholly different material.

Anything you do from the heart enriches you, but sometimes not till years later.

The neurotic has more generous impulses than the normal person, and more mean ones; he just has more impulses.

Happiness is like the penny candy of our youth: we got a lot more for our money back when we had no money.

The payday of those working for you rolls around twice as fast as your own.

My right hand knows what my left hand is doing, but is too fine to do it.

It's hypocrisy if you plan to gain by it, kindness if it's only to spare the feelings of others, tact if it's a little of both.

There are tremendous bargains to be had at auctions, if you like sets of dishes that are mainly soup plates.

Plan for masochists: pay now, live later.

No problem of any consequence can be tackled head on.

The neurotic doesn't know how to cope with his emotional bills; some he keeps paying over and over, others he never pays at all.

Others settle for small rewards; the neurotic must always go for broke.

We are like people with short-term leases on summer cottages: we can never seem to make our provisions come out with our stay.

Young lovers and young nations face the same problem: after orgasm, what?

Neurotics love being in debt; it proves that someone trusts them.

Neurotics are always afraid of missing something: a remark, a reward, a reprieve.

Most of us are impetuously generous just as often as we are impetuously stingy.

Cash is the one gift everyone despises and no one turns down.

∽

Philosophy teaches a man that he can't take it with him; taxes teach him he can't leave it behind either.

What to do with a windfall: spend a little, save a little, gamble a little, pay some bills with what's left.

Furniture dealer: one who will offer to buy your best Edwardian chest for the price you had hoped to get for the kitchen table.

When you let money speak for you, it drowns out anything else you meant to say.

A high salary is the slender thread that many a neurotic ego hangs by.

Money is much more exciting than anything it buys.

There are a handful of people whom money won't spoil, and we all count ourselves among them.

There's nothing quite so maddening to a woman as to be prepared to spend too much for a new dress, and then to not be able to find one.

If you have money, just assume people are after it, and go on from there.

Advice to shopkeepers, restaurant owners, et al.: wildly overcharge; then when you lose a customer, it needn't wound your *amour-propre.*

We're all born brave, trusting, and greedy, and most of us remain greedy.

Money is such a nice, clean, tellable, interesting thing to be worried about.

Even the most extravagant people have one thing they're terribly thrifty about—usually stamps.

I never throw good money after bad; my money has no morality.

We look forward to Christmas, forgetting from one year to the next how expensive and disappointing it was.

When you lose your money, you find out who your friends are—and they're not the ones you wanted.

Most people live within, or beyond, their income, to the same exact percentage, no mater how greatly the income itself varies.

Money is an expensive way to get rid of people, but cheapest in the long run.

When real pleasures fade, there's always the stock market.

Money: in its absence we are coarse; in its presence, we are vulgar.

I wish I'd said it first, and I don't even know who did: The only problems that money can solve are money problems.

Neurotics look on sex and money as just two more weapons.

Those without money often say they would do anything for it, when all they mean is that they would do anything pleasant and convenient. That's why only the rich are rich.

For the most selfish and happy life: spend all your money on yourself when you're young, then on your children as you grow older.

Too much money is as demoralizing as too little, and there's no such thing as exactly enough.

The habit of saving money is hard to acquire, and even harder to break.

How to enter an expensive restaurant: look as though you just bought it.

If you put your money where your mouth is, you're going to have awfully green teeth.

Anything you lose automatically doubles in value.

If you charge it, all children and most women will think it doesn't cost anything.

✍ ✍ ✍

10. Years, Fears, and Other Follies

One day you are an apprentice, and everybody's pet; the next, you are coldly expected to deliver. There is never sufficient warning that the second day is coming.

In youth we are plagued by desire; in later years the desire to feel desire.

It's hard to feel middle-aged, because how can you tell how long you are going to live?

When I was a child, nobody died; but now it happens all the time.

The uses of a dictionary: at thirteen we look up lewd, licentious, and lascivious; at thirty, febrile and inchoate; at fifty, endostosis.

Don't fool yourself that important things can be put off till tomorrow; they can be put off forever, or not at all.

The neurotic longs to touch bottom, so at least he won't have that to worry about any more.

At thirty we are finally free to do everything forbidden to us a thirteen—but God, what a sell!

As the twig is bent, the tree won't grow.

Between a man and a woman both aged fifty there are two full generations, for she might well wed a man in his seventies, and he a girl of twenty.

I have seen messed-up people of forty who still seemed salvageable, and children of six or seven who almost surely were not.

We have a terror of seeming to exert ourselves, lest it be noticed that we exerted ourselves and did not succeed.

The cow is in the meadow, whether we perceive her or not; this is the viewpoint of humility, and middle age brings us to it.

In every group of intimidated people, each thinks "I will rebel," but each waits for the others.

The young have such fervor: nothing can stop them except success.

I envy those whose troubles can be told to others.

We know very little of what we think we know. But fortunately we know quite a lot that we didn't know we knew.

Neurotics excel at counter-espionage, and at inventing espionage to counter.

Mumps, measles, and puppy love are terrible after twenty.

The prime of life: a few slippery years between too-young and too-old.

There is always some specific moment when we realize our youth is gone; but years after, we know it was much later.

My thoughts, I guess, are bitter: who but the bitter have thoughts?

It would be odd, after Manhattan, to live in a place where there were no parades.

Being the youngest always seems such fun, except to the one who is.

The two unhappiest years in a woman's life: when she's thirteen, and when her daughter is.

At Schrafft's, an old lady spoke of her dog: "I woke up in the middle of the night and I thought, my God, suppose he should die before I do."

The past is rich in lessons from which we would greatly profit except that the present is always so full of Special Circumstances.

There are whole years for which I hope I'll never be cross-examined, for I could not give an alibi.

Despair is only the symptom; God knows what the disease is.

The very young and the very old sit way up close to the television set.

The soul may sleep and the body still be happy, but only in youth.

The gambling fever, once it has passed, is as impossible to remember as pain.

What a shame that allowances have to stop with the teens: both those that are paid to us and those that are made for us.

A woman telling her true age is like a buyer confiding his final price to an Armenian rug dealer.

Age is a slowing down of everything except fear.

Traditions are group efforts to keep the unexpected from happening.

To smoke or not to smoke: I can make of either a life-work.

We sometimes feel that we have been really understood, but it was always long ago, by someone now dead.

If it's made of chopped chicken, they now call it a chickenburger—but what if it's made of chopped ham?

The neurotic is always half-drowning in anxiety, and always being half-rescued.

Anxiety is that condition in which, waiting for the unspeakable, we face the undoable.

We all spend our lives in solitary confinement, but the neurotic believes he's the only one.

Much of the time we just tread water, for the raft is too far away and we have gotten tired of swimming.

The past has a form, and perhaps the future will, but the present is always shapeless.

How strange that the young should always think the world is against them—when in fact that is the only time it is for them.

The fear of being laughed at makes cowards of us all.

The neurotic hears others speak of fear, and thinks: You do not know the meaning of the word.

What you were sure of yesterday, you know now to be false, but what you are sure of today is absolutely true.

The past is strapped to our backs. We do not have to see it; we can always feel it.

Throughout our lives, we see in the mirror the same innocent, trusting face we have seen there since childhood.

∽

There are so many things that we wish we had done yesterday, so few that we feel like doing today.

A car is useless in New York, essential everywhere else. The same with good manners.

I've been observing, and have just come to a momentous conclusion: young love owes its life to the invention of tickling.

The two main hazards of psychoanalysis: that it might fail, and that if it succeeds, you'll never be able to forgive yourself for all those wasted years.

Today's music always sounds so cheesy to those who knew yesterday's.

In the bright lexicon of youth, there is no such word as "Yes."

Time-wasters a few decades ago were reading junky novels, which time-wasters today are watching old movies of, on television.

Luck: when your burst of energy doesn't run afoul of somebody else's.

Vengefulness is self-pity's first cousin, loneliness its favorite climate, whiskey its best friend.

The young quickly learn to love and be loved, to betray and be betrayed. The only further lesson maturity can teach them is how to keep from paying too high a price.

We're charmed by coincidence, except when it inconveniences us.

The main difference between the tortured adolescent and the well-adjusted adult: the former's aghast to find that his mind is a cesspool; the latter accepts the fact that everyone's is.

Most neurotics die natural deaths, but they never thought they would.

The young can seldom be faithless for long to the same person.

Spring, summer, and fall fill us with hope; winter alone reminds us of the human condition.

Flesh goes on pleasuring us, and humiliating us, right to the end.

Indignation keeps many people alive, and even keeps some of them young.

Neurotics think of the past with resentment and the future with dread; the present just doesn't exist.

When the salt has lost its savor, pepper makes a poor substitute.

If there's one celebrity at the party, he'll spend the whole time with his clique; if there are two, they'll spend the whole time with each other.

The sophisticate is always haughty when being introduced to a celebrity.

Cigarettes are all the clock I need: one pack finishes the morning, another the afternoon, a third the night.

Your life is made up of years that mean nothing, moments that mean all.

If you jot down every silly thought that pops into your head, you will soon find out everything you most seriously believe.

Aside to women who own jewelry: make a will, leaving each piece to a different young friend or relative. This is a very simple way of assuring yourself a little immortality. (Like Cyril Connolly, I define immortality as ten years.)

On the first day of spring there was a terrible snowstorm, and I felt I should atone for something.

The young couldn't care less about what people over thirty think.

The neurotic listens to weather reports about Small Craft Warnings, and he thinks: They're talking about me.

Loneliness, insomnia, and change: the fear of these is even worse than the reality.

There's no such thing as the Right Person, unless it's the Right Time.

For neurotics, success is a five-minute wonder; failure a five-year plan.

It's innocence when it charms us, ignorance when it doesn't.

People have to be very old to die one at a time; young, they take a lot of others with them.

A face that's full of delight is per se a delightful face—except of course on television.

I know which side my bread is buttered on: the side which falls on the carpet.

Regardless of circumstances, a man never breaks off with a pretty woman who causes him absolutely no trouble.

A neurotic is afraid to see himself as he's afraid others see him.

I have an understanding with my husband: on any day when I haven't done any writing, I must play him three games of chess. The trouble is, if I have been working, I enjoy the chess; if not, all I want to play is Russian roulette.

Fine feathers make fine birds, until it comes time to fly.

I've started keeping files, so at last I'm methodical: I now know exactly how many months I let letters go unanswered.

Our strength is often composed of the weakness we're damned if we're going to show.

The human comedy can keep amusing you, but only if you keep your distance.

The neurotic's boat keeps drifting farther and farther out to sea, and people keep asking him why he's so nervous.

"Let's cut 'em off at the pass." This is frequently done to the villains in Westerns, and to the rest of us in real life.

If you let a situation get bad enough, every word you say will only make it worse.

It's the most unhappy people who most fear change.

People determined to hide their feelings are usually non-stop talkers.

Why are people surprised when nice girls get into trouble? The ones who aren't nice know better.

Neurotics expect you to remember all the things that they tell you, and many that they didn't.

Vanity, revenge, loneliness, boredom, all apply: lust is one of the least of the reasons for promiscuity.

Some hungry newspapers feed exclusively on scare headlines, and so do some hungry people.

Whether or not you love television, you've got to admit it certainly loves itself.

Recipe I've hit on, for a wonderful life: at least once a month, do something exciting that you've never done before. And please let me know how it comes out.

The young spend their time, *faute de mieux*, practicing on each other; but they don't want the old practicing on them too.

I'm glad I don't have to explain to a man from Mars why each day I set fire to dozens of little pieces of paper, and put them in my mouth.

Sing it loud and clear: there's no vinism like chauvinism.

Each new non-prescription sleeping pill proudly advertises: "It's not habit-forming"—which naturally means go ahead and take it 365 nights a year.

Epitaph for the human race: We've been terrible, but dear God how we've paid for it.

CPSIA information can be obtained
at www.ICGtesting.com
Printed in the USA
BVHW08s1254190918
527933BV00030B/1506/P